the
clothesline

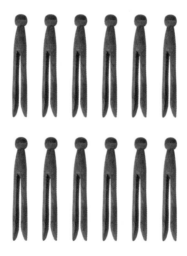

the
clothesline

IRENE RAWLINGS   ANDREA VANSTEENHOUSE

WITH PHOTOGRAPHY BY

DAVID FOXHOVEN & JASON McCONATHY

GIBBS SMITH

Gibbs Smith, Publisher

First Edition
06 05 04   5 4 3 2

Published by
Gibbs Smith, Publisher
P.O. Box 667
Layton, Utah 84041

Order toll-free: (1-800) 748-5439
www.gibbs-smith.com

Edited by Suzanne Gibbs Taylor
Designed and produced by Loneta Showell
Printed and bound in Hong Kong

Library of Congress Cataloging-in-Publication Data

Rawlings, Irene.
  The clothesline / Irene Rawlings and Andrea VanSteenhouse ;
photographs by David Foxhoven and Jason McConathy.— 1st ed.
    p. cm.
  ISBN 1-58685-143-8
  1. Laundry. I. Van Steenhouse, Andrea. II. Title.
  TT985 .R39 2002
  648'.1—dc21
                    2001008053

Contents

We Finally Come Clean

For thousands of years, people hauled their laundry to the river, pounded the clothes on rocks, and spread them out on bushes to dry. The harder they pounded, the cleaner their clothes became. Things changed dramatically with the invention of soap sometime around 500 B.C. Some historians say the Phoenicians invented soap by accidentally mixing goat fat with ash. Others credit this miraculous invention to the ancient Egyptians who, as part of their daily wardrobe, wore cakes of perfumed tallow on their heads. So it makes sense that some of it, as it melted and dripped, would mix with the ash of banked household fires. The real question is, who thought to use this gooey mixture of fat and ash to wash clothes?

Centuries passed and nothing much changed in the wash-day routine until the Age of Enlightenment in the 1600s. The English and French deserve equal credit for civilizing the process of washing clothes by hiring battalions of servants and devoting entire rooms in their country manors and chateaux to soaping, soaking, boiling, ironing, and folding clothes. Those who could not afford servants still benefited from laborsaving devices like the "pounder," a stout stick capped by a block of wood. When moved up and down in the washtub, the pounder created a sucking and swirling motion similar to the action of the modern washing machine.

Clotheslines and clothespins came along in the 1800s. We're guessing (but think we're not far off the mark) that the idea for using rope to hang clothes was borrowed by an inventive housewife from her seafaring husband. Clothespins followed. First came the push kind we now think of as the knob-top, originally whittled by hand with fanciful bird and floral tops. The spring or clip kind was first patented in 1832. According to U.S. Patent Office records, more than 150 clothespin models were patented between 1840 and 1887.

When we were growing up—Andrea in California and I in Michigan—backyards on wash day were full of promise and revelations. One glance at a clothesline told everything about the new family down the block—did they have boys or girls? Did they use plain or fancy sheets? My sheets were always sensible white cotton, so I really wanted to be friends with any little girl who had sheets with a Raggedy Ann or Cinderella print. We didn't realize that our mothers were also making up their minds about the new folks in town, based on the way they hung their clothesline. This is how the love affair with laundry lines started for us.

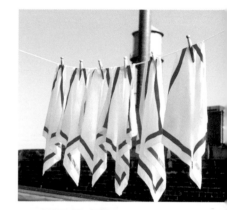

Although each of our homes is equipped with washer and dryer, we rarely pass up a chance to hang clothes up on the line. Nothing beats the smell of clothes dried in fresh air and sunshine.

Andrea: Laborsaving devices introduced in the 1940s and 1950s were supposed to give homemakers more leisure time. Now, more than fifty years later, we discover that we don't have any more time than our mothers and grandmothers did three decades ago. Perhaps even less. Or, maybe what we're doing with that time is less satisfying.

In any case, everyone is in a hurry. Everyone is busy, over-scheduled, overstressed in jobs where we don't often see a concrete result. So, we long for a simpler time when people were more connected to one another—by extended family, by neighborhoods, by communities, and by the simple tasks that sustained life and gave it continuity.

These tasks were repeated weekly—washing, ironing, baking bread. The sounds and smells associated with each of these tasks give me a warm feeling that all is well with the world. Now, even though I don't need to, I re-create these tasks to feel a connection

with my mother and grandmother. Hanging out the wash gives me a window into the lives of the women who came before and makes my own life more meaningful.

Over the years I have come to realize that, throughout shocking political and cultural upheavals, one thing that connects women over the generations is the making and tending of cloth. For me, washing, mending, and folding the clothes of my children kept me in physical touch with the stages of their lives.

Irene: Clotheslines were a big part of my growing-up years (that's me in the photo above) and the picture of them, heavy in all seasons with my family's clothes, is as vivid a memory as my mother's panicky cry, "Hurry, hurry, it's going to rain. Hurry. Help me bring in the clothes." We'd rush out under the darkening sky to pull in the blouses, underwear, sheets, and towels my mother had painstakingly pegged up on the line, and if we were really lucky, we'd have all the clothes inside before those first enormous raindrops splashed and exploded against the windows.

I don't hang laundry out in the winter as my mother did, but as soon as the icicle carrots have melted from the eaves of my house, I think of two things: planting a garden and hanging the laundry outside. My washing goes out on the line as soon as the pale sun can sustain a few hours of warmth. The simple act of picking clean, wet clothes out of a wicker basket, shaking them out, and hanging them up makes me slow down, giving me time to compose the rest of my day.

In times gone by, many women kept a domestic diary. It was a ledger of remedies and recipes for everything from making soap to removing stains from fine linens. These diaries were passed down from mother to daughter for generations and are not only a practical compendium of household hints but also an encyclopedia of correct behavior.

We were lucky enough to find a well-thumbed household diary in a thrift store. Started in 1906, it was used and added to until the mid-1940s. The yellowed, splotchy pages attest to the many years of good use.

The most endearing part of this book talks about washing clothes. The early entries are written in now-faded pencil and the later ones are typed on a Remington portable. There are detailed directions for making clothespin bags (". . . use cotton ticking to make wide and shallow pockets . . .") and ironing board pads (". . . use heavy silence cloth, the kind used to protect your dining table . . . do not use old blankets").

Wash-day hints include recipes for wash-day foods, suggesting something hearty but good served cold, like buttermilk fried chicken or boiled meat. Ironing-day recipe suggestions include stewed meat and bread but "nothing with a strong odor like onions because it will spoil the smell of the wash." Each of the recipes in the diary was considered quick and easy in its own day.

And, of course, there's a lot about the actual hanging of the household laundry. This reads not only as an ironclad set of instructions but also as a social commentary. How you hung laundry on the line told the neighborhood of your womanly abilities.

One of the earliest entries prohibits hanging undergarments outdoors. An indoor line "strung up next to the furnace is the proper place to dry your corsets, stockings and pantlets." An entry from the 1920s suggests a unique method of dealing with prying neighbors. ". . . hang your silk underwear up inside a pillowcase where it will dry nicely but not be exposed to direct sunlight."

We met Bessie and her mother in the pages of this diary. They kept meticulous notes about running a household but also made entries about small-town life, church suppers, and family values. We also found, tucked in among the pages, letters they had written—short and to the point but full of love and mother-daughter advice.

a few basic shapes

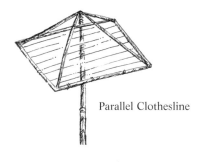

Parallel Clothesline

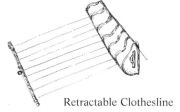

Retractable Clothesline

T-Post Clothesline

Umbrella Clothesline

2 qt grease
1 qt water
1 can lye
1/4 cup ammonia
3 tbs borax
Hazel's Soap Recipe

Making soap was a time-consuming part of the wash-day routine in grandma's day—and dangerous too . . . judging from the recipes we discovered in the diary.

We found a simple soap recipe dating from the 1940s, did a little experimenting, and came up with this quick and easy recipe for making lemon verbena and lavender soap. We found this recipe works with most other culinary herbs or herb combinations, so you may want to experiment to create your own special scent.

> 12 oz. of unscented soap (approx. three cakes)
> $1^1/2$ teaspoons sweet almond oil
> 1 teaspoon dried lemon verbena, finely crumbled or chopped
> 6 drops lemon verbena essential oil
> 6 drops lavender essential oil

Finely grate the unscented soap with a cheese grater. Put into a double boiler over low heat. Heat, stirring occasionally. Gradually the soap will melt into a thick paste. Add the sweet almond oil and the dried herbs. Transfer the mixture to a clean, nonreactive bowl. Add the essential oils and mix thoroughly with a wooden spoon.

For soap bars: Pour it immediately into a wax-lined container like a cut-down paper milk carton. After it hardens (about a week), slice it into squares with a sharp knife.

For soap balls: When mixture is cool enough to handle, shape into round balls with your hands. Put the balls on a cookie sheet covered with parchment paper to harden. Make sure you won't need the cookie sheet for four or five days, which is how long it will take the soap balls to harden. This recipe makes approximately three four-ounce balls.

Most of us have fond memories of clotheslines and the simpler times they represent. Over the past five years, we've traveled around the United States and Canada peeking into backyards, photographing clotheslines, and talking with people. Everyone with whom we discussed this book—friends, well-known authors, poets, artists, environmentalists, mothers, and grandmothers—offered their thoughts and recollections. They sent us copies of old family recipes for removing grass stains and told us about the time the cat unraveled an entire sweater hung out on the line to dry. We also tasted recipes for wash-day suppers like green tomato casserole and—our favorite—catfish on a plank. We received too much stuff to put into the book so . . . we've set up a website (**www.theclotheslinebook.com**) where you can read recipes and recollections, stories and poetry. But here's the best part—we've created a virtual back fence over which you can share your own clothesline memories with other readers who also love the sunny smell and crisp feel of line-dried laundry.

My grandma's clotheslines in winter
Were often encased in glazed icicles of sleet
Or stiffened by the north wind of poverty
Blowing fright on the lower middle class

It never would have occurred to them
To sleep late, cut a corner, wash some other day
What had to be done got done—numbed
Fingers folded the new week's rectitude.

by Robert N. Wilson

If you wash on Monday, you have all the week to dry . . .
If you wash on Tuesday, you're still not much awry . . .
If you wash on Friday, you wash in real need . . .
If you wash on Saturday, you are slovenly indeed.

From an early 1900s skip-rope rhyme

clotheslines

Everyone washes and dries clothes. Most of us have early memories of clotheslines and of the simpler times they represent. Even people who don't hang their clothes out have fond feelings for a time when towels hung out on the line smelled like spring.

What is a clothesline? A clothesline can be colorful Amish quilts hanging out on the front porch of an Iowa farmhouse, a decades-old skirted bathing suit drying on a rusty nail in a Maine summer house, a long row of dish towels haphazardly hung on a ranch house line, wool socks drying on a steam radiator in a tiny New York walk-up, white sheets flapping furiously in a fierce prairie wind that comes just before the rain, or blue jeans frozen stiff on a wintry line in Montana.

Hanging laundry on a line is one of life's luxuries. It represents time. Time to be alone. Time to think, even to meditate, accompanied by the repeated actions of hanging clothes—stooping, straightening, lifting, hanging, breathing, watching the clouds. There is a spirituality in the simple, positive actions of this everyday activity.

Not Just for the Laundry

Clotheslines are not just for drying laundry. You can string lines to hold photos, notes, invitations, or holiday cards. Hang a line along a wall for an instant and easily updatable art gallery of children's drawings. Any kind of string or covered wire works as a handy place to hang reminders of appointments, interior-design ideas clipped from magazines, or small swatches of fabric being considered for pillows or curtains. In a sewing room, hang patterns, sketches, and little needlework projects in progress (put each in its own colorful paper shopping bag) to keep them out of the way but within easy reach.

In farmhouse kitchens from Maine to Texas, frugal housewives used lengths of string (held up by screw eyes or, in some cases, color-coordinated thumbtacks) as curtain rods. This simple, effective way of hanging window curtains can give the kitchen or bathroom of your cabin or cottage a vintage 1930s or 1940s look.

Patriotism is displayed on a weathered clothesline—a special way to savor our favorite symbols.

Washing: Yellowing from age can be removed by soaking the linens in cold water for a few days, changing the water as needed, then carefully handwashing with a mild soap. For stubborn stains, soak linens in a solution of one part water to one part lemon juice mixed with a well-dissolved pinch of salt. Gently handwash.

CLEANING VINTAGE LINENS

Drying: Roll in a towel to remove excess moisture and then dry flat. Spread linens out on a fragrant bush such as lilac or lavender, allowing the sun to bleach them while they dry.

Pressing: Press linens while slightly damp, using a pressing cloth to prevent scorching.

What Clotheslines Say About Us

Throughout time, clotheslines have said something about how we lived. Lots of little things hung on the line meant there were lots of little children. Workshirts and overalls said there was a laborer in the house. White shirts and dozens of handkerchiefs meant an office worker. A woman who hung her laundry by color, by size, and by kind was considered a good woman. A woman whose line was hung haphazardly was considered an indifferent housekeeper. Someone who hung her underwear out for everyone to see was a hussy. Even now, when we pass a full clothesline, we take a furtive glance to see if the underwear is plain, serviceable cotton, or a frivolous lace.

Women learned to hang laundry "the right way" from their mothers, who operated with the absolute certainty that there was a proper way to hang laundry.

Today, clotheslines weighted with wet laundry flapping jauntily in the wind still say something about us. Perhaps they say we don't want to use a dryer, or we simply like to sleep on sheets that smell of fresh air and newly cut grass, or we like to dry ourselves with towels that are satisfyingly scratchy.

Is this a collection of formerly loved dresses, ones to pass along to someone else? Or is this a hopeful gathering of last spring's comfort clothes asking if they are still in favor this year? The leisurely pace of hanging laundry on a line gives us the time to carefully consider such questions.

Summer's Lines

Summerhouse clotheslines are different from all others. The boundaries between inside and outside are blurred. The clotheslines are more uncontrived and haphazard. Summerhouse clotheslines are full of towels and bathing suits, sheets, pillowcases, and cotton blankets from beds stripped after the weekend guests have departed.

In the 1940s, the J. R. Watkins Company—manufacturers of soap flakes, perfumed starch, and other household products—published a book of household hints. It included tips like "If your summer schedule does not allow you to iron linens while they are still damp off the line, loosely roll the damp linens in a clean muslin fabric and store for up to a day. If you forget and the linens develop little black mildew dots, blend soap, powdered starch, salt and the juice of one lemon. Rub stains on both sides of the material and place in the sun. Repeat if necessary. Then wash with hot water and soap."

Honeysuckle vines shift in the wind, and their magic scent drifts up onto the screen porch. Simple surroundings allow us to relax in the uncommon elegance of quiet solitude, and we listen to towels and pillowcases flapping gently in the breeze as we prepare for an afternoon nap out on the porch.

Dolls and stuffed animals should be washed by hand in warm water, using a gentle soap or detergent. Washing stuffed toys in the machine, even on the gentle cycle, will cause the stuffing to shift, and the toy will get a lumpy, uneven look.

WASHING STUFFED TOYS

Add a pinch of borax (available in grocery stores and drugstores) to the washing water to preserve colors. A pinch of salt in the rinse water will also help keep colors fresh and bright.

Add a drop of essential oil (lavender or lemon verbena) to the rinse water for a long-lasting good smell. A pinch of powdered orrisroot is another good choice.

Line-dry the stuffed toys in sunlight.

Children, Dolls & Clotheslines

The most treasured possessions of our childhood eventually need the special touch of gentle soap and a soft breeze. A six-year-old asking her mother, "How can I wash my Ann? Will her hair color change?" may define an entire afternoon. Many years later the child, now herself the mother of a six-year-old asking the same questions, recalls that afternoon and says, "We'll just dissolve a little borax in the washing water to keep Ann's hair nice and bright. Then we'll hang her out on the line to dry in the sun."

Adding just a pinch of powdered orrisroot—the kind available in craft stores as a fixative for potpourri—to the washing water along with the borax gives a delicate, pleasant scent to much-loved dolls and stuffed animals.

Even in this easy-care age, little girls still take the time to wash their doll clothes.

If your children enjoy helping with the wash, designate an area in the laundry room where they can scrub and splash to their hearts' content.

To make their wash water soapy (but not overly so), take a bar of gentle soap, put it into the toe of a clean pair of old panty hose and swirl it around in the wash water. Have another bowl or basin ready for rinsing.

Dear Mother,

I want to ask you about washing the bedding. First you soak them in warm water. You dissolve some soap to put in this, don't you? How much? Then when you wash the clothes the first time, do you use the water in which they were soaked or do you wring them out of this and use all clean water?

We lost money on the sale of our honey but are having a good apple crop for cider.

Your loving daughter, Bessie

Dear Bessie,

Make a lather of good soap with very hot water. And let it cool until it is lukewarm. Then let the blankets and coverlets soak in it for a while. Then take a new clean hoe for a pounder. Pound well and pound again in another suds. Rinse thoroughly and hang on the line without wringing. If a hose is handy, spray plenty of water over them when they are hanging out on the line.

Your loving mother

O ur mothers and grandmothers did the washing by hand and hung it out on the line every Monday of their adult lives—come rain or hail or frost or snow. Even marryings and buryings didn't much alter this time-validated ritual. As little girls, they practiced for this role by washing, drying, and ironing their doll clothes.

Hang personal items on the inside lines so as to thwart the curiosity of nosy neighbors

The virtues of hanging a "proper line" are part of the laundry lore passed down through the generations. Mothers advised their daughters not to hang undergarments outdoors so as to not encourage the neighbors' curiosity. Another maternal suggestion: hang personal items outdoors but on the inside lines, surrounded by sheets or other large items to thwart the gawking of nosy neighbors.

Vintage laundry bags made from brightly dyed cotton fade with constant exposure to sun, wind, and rain. Contemporary laundry bags, like the Martha Stewart design pictured on the *right*, are often made out of Sunbrella® or other acrylic outdoor fabrics, which are sturdy enough to withstand the elements without fading.

Colorful Clothespin Bags & White Huck Towels

Most books of household hints from the 1900s include directions on making clothespin bags. Sometimes these bags were made from two pieces of heavy unbleached muslin, but more often a housewife chose to express her creativity by making this utilitarian object out of colorful floursacking material. Another popular design was made by sewing up the bottom of a little girl's dress. Today's clothespin bags, often with a retro look, are made from weather-resistant fabrics.

Many of the tips found in these slim volumes are charmingly outdated, while others are remarkably contemporary. You might want to try this one: "In cold weather if towels are rinsed in salt water after being washed, they will not freeze on the line. Bring them in and, without ironing, fold and put away. Salt is particularly good for bath towels, as the salt left in the towel is exhilarating for the skin when used after a bath."—*Audel's Household Helps, Hints and Receipts, 1913.*

The Dishes are Done

A dishtowel gets more use than any other piece of cloth in the house. It is used to dry dishes, to do a little light dusting, to pick up spills, and occasionally to grip a hot pot handle on the stove.

To stand up to hard use and constant washing, the dish towels you buy should be pure cotton. A cotton blend will not be as absorbent and, although they look great when you buy them, will quickly pill up in the wash. For drying glasses and stemware, linen towels work best because they don't leave any fibers behind on the glass. Towels dried on the line benefit from a natural bleaching by the sun and get a fresh scent from the breeze.

Striped dishtowels hang on the line at Avalanche Ranch in the Colorado Rockies. The dry mountain air and bright sunshine make short work (about ten minutes) of the drying process.

A Place at the Table

Floral cotton tablecloths, once the workhorse of everyday dinners all across America (white damask was saved for special occasions), are now highly collectible. Tablecloths in good condition fetch high prices in antiques shops all across the country and on eBay. Unfortunately, most of these colorful table coverings come marked with the memories of many meals. Removing the stains after so many years is not easy.

We've found some old folk recipes for removing the most stubborn stains. Our recipes are organic, but that doesn't mean that working with them won't be hard on your hands. Use rubber gloves to keep the lemon juice and salt out of any small cuts. Fortunately, cotton and linen fibers are sturdy enough to withstand hot temperatures and tough laundry treatments, although colors may fade.

Coffee, tea, and fruit stains are easily removed by putting the stained tablecloth over the sink and pouring boiling water over the stain. Repeat.

RECIPES FOR REMOVING STAINS

To remove grease, make a paste of granulated sugar and water. Rub it into the stain and let it set before washing. Dry in the sun.

For rust, make a paste of lemon juice and salt and apply to the spot. Put the fabric in the sun or hold it over steam until the stain disappears.

Scorch, if not too brown, will disappear if dipped in borax and water, and then dried in the sun.

To remove wax, first harden (using ice cubes). Scrape off excess with a dull table knife. For washable fabric, stretch over a bowl and pour boiling water through the stain. For non-washables, place between several layers of clean white cotton or muslin fabric and press with a warm iron.

The sounds and smells of summer suppers outdoors are included in our fondest childhood recollections—spaghetti with meatballs and runny red sauce, great potato salads, baked beans cooked for hours with molasses and salt pork, and rhubarb pies. Unfortunately, the tablecloths became marked with the memories of each event, but our mothers knew all the tricks to take the stains out.

Mood Indigo

Blue jeans are the universal symbol of work and their patches are the mark of thrift. Like old soldiers standing at attention, these jeans don't die; they just fade. Even now they convey their readiness to ride the wind and command the resilient fabric to be sturdy, strong, and dependable.

Their weight on the clothesline is impressive and demanding. As if calling attention to their importance, they take as long as they wish to dry—sometimes all day.

Grandma used metal stretchers, bought at the hardware store, that she put inside the wet jeans to stretch them into shape.

To remove grass stains, sponge them with rubbing alcohol or soak in a solution of 2 tablespoons ammonia mixed with 1 cup water. Rinse in cool water. Launder as usual.

BLUE JEANS HINTS

Blue jeans should be hung on the line dripping wet. This prevents wrinkles so the jeans won't need ironing. When dry, press inside out, if necessary.

Put a pinch of salt in the rinse water when washing a new pair of jeans. This will keep their color bright.

Dear Mother,
Should I use hot water for washing?
My neighbor says it sets stains.
We are going on a car-camping trip.
I will send you photographs.

Your loving daughter, Bessie

Dear Bessie,
Scalding water sets stains while briskly boiling removes them.
Pour boiling water through stained laundry and all discoloration will be removed if you have not let it set in a previous washing.

Your loving mother

White clothes should be left on the line as long as possible; colored clothes should be brought in out of the sun as soon as they are dry.

Grandma knew the bleaching properties of sunshine and left her whites on the line all day. To whiten clothes that became yellow from too much soap and not enough rinsing, she used a recipe passed down from her mother: "Wash clothes as usual. Then dissolve cream of tartar in cool water (1 teaspoon per quart). Soak clothes overnight. Dry on the line." It still works. Your whites—towels, sheets, or shirts—will be as white as new.

WASHING OLD LINENS

To wash old linen towels, add one-half cup mild detergent (Ivory Snow® or Dreft® are good) and 2 table-spoons white vinegar to 2 quarts very cold water. Dunk repeatedly in the water but do not soak. Rinse in clean, cold water. Hang up to dry.

After allowing the linens to damp-dry in the sunshine, fold them into a cotton sheet and let them stand for about an hour. Then, stretch the still slightly damp linens by tugging on the opposite corners to bring them back to square. For larger linens, like tablecloths, you will need the help of an assistant. Children will love helping with this task, which resembles a gentle game of tug-o-war.

Using special family linens brings happiness to our hearts and loveliness to our homes. When we hand-wash our best linens and hang them out with loving care, we can re-create the smell and feel of grandma's house.

Preserving Heirloom Linens

Handmade linen and lace are highly cherished items. If you are fortunate enough to own some heirloom linens, proper care is very important. Traditional recipes called for rainwater mixed with white castile soap in warm water, followed by repeated rinsing. Today's homekeeper can achieve the same results by using a mild soap in cold water. If your linens are very fragile, first line your washbasin with an old bath towel, which will act like a little protective hammock when you take the linens out of the water. Blot dry with fresh towels (use as many as you need) until just damp. Hang over a towel on the line to dry.

The Familiar Rituals

Clotheslines—in the backyard, on the front porch, or over the alley— were meeting places for women to share recipes, remedies, and closely held secrets. Before automatic washers and gas dryers, women started their work early and moved quickly to finish the day's chores before dark. At the clothesline, in the safety of the familiar daily rituals, women shared questions and concerns, dreams and expectations, and recipes for banana cream pie—all to the rhythm of cleansing and renewing the fabric that clothed their families.

Simple Line—Elegant Decor

The Paris-apartment feel of this bedroom was created by combining romantic fabrics with soft lighting. The clothesline—strung between the bedposts of a metal four-poster bed—has draped over it a vintage silk-chiffon scarf printed with lilacs, tea-dyed cotton gloves, and a hand-embroidered glove bag. Although they have been positioned on the line with care, they are meant to convey a certain nonchalance.

To get the look, don't be afraid to combine flea-market finds with serious antiques. Dust off and display your family portraits and refurbish grandma's silk lampshades. Layer your room with opulent fabrics—velvets, silks, chiffons. Make poofy, lace-edged pillows or simply drape some vintage fabric over a clothesline and hang on the wall or string between the bedposts.

To wash silk, put ¼ cup mild detergent and 2 tablespoons white vinegar in 2 quarts very cold water. Wash gently. Rinse. Roll in a heavy towel. Iron while still damp.

WASHING & STORING DELICATES

Hand-washed lace and silk will have extra luster if you use half milk and half water for the final rinse.

Wash velvet by gently swirling it in warm sudsy water. Rinse several times. Don't squeeze or twist. Hang on the line to drip dry. A little breeze or soft brush will bring up the nap when it is dry.

Store fragile fabrics rolled up, not folded. If they are going to be stored for a long time, make sure all the starch or sizing is washed out of them first.

How Clothespins Started

The first American clothespin patent was issued in 1832 and was quickly followed by many adaptations of its simple but effective design. Wooden clothespins are made from maple, white birch, pine, or oak. In the early 1900s, sailors on long whaling voyages made scrimshaw clothespins for their sweethearts.

To make a new clothesline last longer, soak it in hot water. When thoroughly dry, rub with a little liquid wax (like Pledge®). Let wax dry completely before hanging any clothes. This keeps the line pliable and makes it waterproof.

THE LINE & THE PINS

To make clothespins last longer, put into boiling water and oil them for a few minutes. Dry quickly. Do this once a month.

Taut Lines and a Fair Wind

White fabric isn't "white" in its original state. Unbleached cotton fabrics, known to the trade as "gray goods," are yellowish in color. Raw wool, even from the whitest fleece, is a creamy color.

Before these fabrics are made into sheets, shirts, towels, and linens, they are bleached by the manufacturer. Then they are blued.

After the fabric is used, the bleach and bluing wear and wash off. A little bluing in the last rinse water adds the necessary tint to make your laundry snowy white.

—Mrs. Stewart's Bluing
Housewife's Home Washing Guide, 1943.

On Monday, every housewife prayed for sunshine and a good breeze to dry and gently bleach her laundry. There was a friendly competition among the neighborhood women to see who got her wash out first, and there were ironclad rules to follow: hang taut lines, with the laundry evenly spaced and sorted by color, size, and function; hang socks together and shirts together; everything must be precisely arranged so that even the clothespins stand up in perfect rows like little soldiers. If she did everything right, her neighbors would say, "She hangs a proper line."

The beauty of linens is often in the details. Embroidered flowers or monograms on pillowcases, sheets, napkins, tablecloths and lace-edged huck cloths or handkerchiefs retain their beauty if properly ironed.

IRONING EMBROIDERED LINENS

For best results, iron linens while they are still damp. To preserve and enhance raised embroidery, put a clean white bath towel down on the ironing board and place linens right side down on the padded surface. Press on the wrong side.

Airing the Bedding

Some days are better than others for airing the bedding. Days that dawn bright and promise a purifying sun and a rustling of wind are the best. If your wool blankets need laundering, add a tablespoon of ammonia and a tablespoon of detergent to a large basin of mildly tepid (lukewarm) water. Put a pinch of borax in the washing water to keep colorful blankets from fading. Rinse in cold water. Line dry.

Dear Mother,

There's a little nip in the air, so I'm going to wash my quilts so they will be fresh for winter. You used to beat them, didn't you? But I can't remember why. Henry and the boys send their love.

Your loving daughter, Bessie

Dear Bessie,

I hope you washed all your blankets and quilts in the spring . . . if not, wait for the first snowfall and gently refresh your bedding by rolling it in the powdery snow. Shake off the snow, fluff up the bedding, and let it dry naturally. In spring, after you wash the quilts, fold them over the line and beat to lighten the cotton batting. But don't beat so hard as to break the stitches. I learned this from my own mother—your grandmother.

Your loving mother

The Wild Prairie Wind

Spring. Like the return of dandelions and the first tender sprouts of creeping thyme between the flagstones of the walk, clotheslines are a sign of spring. There's still a bite in the air and the wind is whippy and wild, but clothes hung out on the line will bring indoors with them the very definite smell of spring. Winter laundry, brought indoors to finish drying, smells clean but does not exhale bright yellow sunshine.

City Folks Hang Out Wash, Too

Clotheslines still exist in older urban neighborhoods. If you take the El in Chicago or the New York–New Haven train, you can see cramped, improvised urban laundry lines. Diapers, towels, and underwear are hung up over the balcony rails or up under the overhang to catch any hint of breeze. City folks hang their laundry out to dry on lines strung in the courtyard or air space between apartment buildings or out to telephone poles in the alley.

Urban lines have a different flavor from the expansive lines in the country. They are smaller and more to the point. In cities, sun is often blocked by tall buildings, yet the laundry still hangs, draped like sculpture on the line.

A pair of stiletto-heeled dancing shoes, *left*, hangs out to dry after being caught in a rainstorm. The vintage stainless steel clothespins have that machine-age look. Red-bordered napkins, *facing, right*, blow casually on a roof-top line.

Even Cowboys Use Clothespins

Leather gloves are very important in a cowboy's life to protect his hands from the harsh cold winters riding fences and from rope burns during branding time in the spring. When cowboys have been out in a rainstorm and their gloves have gotten wet, they hang them out to dry on a lead rope in the shelter of the back of a horse trailer. When the gloves are damp-dry, they can be stretched back into shape by simply putting them on and going back to work.

Self-sufficient cowboys out on the range in summer often carry a line and clothespins so they can wash a few "necessaries" without having to go back to the ranch or into town.

To clean white or tan gloves, put them on your hands and douse in rubbing alcohol. Remove gloves and they will dry quickly without odor. Wash your hands thoroughly.

TAKING CARE OF LEATHER

To clean dark leather, mix 1 cup linseed oil with 1 cup white vinegar. Wipe onto dirty leather using a clean cloth. Let stand for a few minutes. Wipe off and polish with a clean soft cloth.

To keep leather soft, rub with a soft cloth dampened in castor oil.

Autumn's Colorful Lines

Autumn is a great season to use a clothesline, but though the sun's color is strong, its drying power is weak. Hang clothes out early in the morning so they can dry all day. Don't worry about colors fading.

The breezes—in this season of briskness, of harvest, of gratitude for warm pajamas and socks and homemade quilts—carry with them the nostalgic smell of distant woodsmoke that lightly perfumes the clothesline.

In the old days, laundry was done in the yard or in laundry rooms stuck away in the basement . . . humid, dark rooms with small windows and a cement floor. Not anymore.

Laundry rooms have become the new thing. Homes are being built with laundry rooms that are large, airy, and welcoming, incorporating the same custom cabinetry and countertops, designer window and floor treatments as the rest of the house. Also important are large work areas, improved storage, and the latest in energy-saving washers and dryers. Ironing boards are usually built-in, and, after decades of plastic, irons have gone back to a hefty professional weight.

When older homes are renovated, the laundry room is no longer an afterthought. It is redecorated—sometimes relocated—to make wash day more convenient.

An Artful Laundry

When friends asked Karen Moore, owner of Djuna (an antiques, art, and fine fabric shop in Denver), to help decorate their newly built mountain home, she was a little surprised to discover that a laundry room was tops on their list. "I learned pretty quickly that laundry rooms are hot," she says.

The room she designed is bright and cheery with two dryers ("drying clothes outside in the winter can be rough," she says) and lots of space to display any of the owners' art that spills over from the rest of the house.

The indigo-blue Mexican-tile countertops coordinate with the gray-blue color of the under-counter drawer fronts and cabinets.

The slate-blue farmhouse sink is deep enough for soaking hand-washables.

Scented fabric softener and ironing water are stored on high shelves that are deep enough to store extra towels.

There's something so satisfying about the fresh, steamy scent of just-ironed linens. And adding the sweet smell of lavender to this mix is a natural. Lavender is

There's something so satisfying about the scent of recently ironed linens.

not only a powerful antibacterial and a natural insecticide but, for centuries, it has been associated with good household management. Handwritten kitchen diaries dating from the nineteenth century recommend tucking a few sprigs of dried lavender in between folded sheets to keep them smelling fresh.

If you plan to store your linens for an extended period of time, it is best to wrap them (laundered, line dried but unironed) in clean white cotton cloth. Acid-free tissue is often recommended for heirloom linens but we prefer using old white cotton or linen sheets.

The simple addition of homemade lavender water to your laundry sprinkler or spray bottle allows this wonderfully fresh scent to fill the air every time you sprinkle or spritz.

MAKING LAVENDER IRONING WATER

3 oz. 90-proof vodka
12 drops lavender essential oil
12 oz. purified water

Sterilize a 16 oz. bottle by boiling for 10 minutes or running through the pot-scrubber cycle in your dishwasher. Pour the vodka into sterilized bottle, add lavender essential oil. Swirl vigorously to mix and let stand for at least 24 hours. Add the purified water. Pour into a spray bottle and enjoy the lavender's refreshing scent while you iron. Store in the refrigerator. Keeps for 6 weeks, then it gradually loses its scent.
CAUTION: Do not use this in a steam iron.

Personalized laundry bags make it easy for family members to pick up their socks and underwear. At the very least, a bag marked "whites" and another marked "darks" make wash day less of a chore. If your laundry room is large enough, using two additional hampers to hold sheets and towels is also a good idea.

A Small, Efficient Space

Just because your laundry room is small doesn't mean it has to be cramped or boring. Designer JoAnne Gadowski of Dynamic Dimensions, located in Denver, Colorado, has created a pretty first-floor laundry room in a rambling, late-nineteenth-century home. Walls are painted a sunny yellow, and windows are left uncurtained except for a sheer valance whose flirty points mirror the whimsical harlequin pattern on the door.

Soaps and scrubs are stored efficiently and attractively in glass jars and galvanized pails. Flat baskets can be used to store fine hand-washables. First line them to keep delicate lace from snagging on the wicker.

Storage for Linens

A closet or armoire full of freshly laundered linens is an object of beauty. Remember not to fold an item the same way after each washing, as this causes stress along the fold lines. Store linens on an open, airy shelf. Don't store vintage linens in a cedar chest because cedar oil can leave stains.

For long-term storage—roll, don't fold. Don't add lavender bags or lavender sprigs because over time their oil can damage fragile fibers. Wrap vintage linens in acid-free paper or clean, old, white, all-cotton or linen sheets.

A small sachet filled with fresh lavender will fill an entire linen closet or armoire with its distinctively pungent scent. This not only makes your linens smell fresh but also helps to repel moths. Tie a few sprigs with a silk ribbon and hang in your closet.

Lavender bags do double duty—repelling moths as they sweetly scent your linens.

If you have lavender growing in your garden, harvest it early in the morning before the dew dries. This is when the flowers have the most fragrance, so they will retain their scent longer.

To refresh a lavender sachet that has gone flat, add just a drop or two of lavender oil to bring back the aroma.

MAKING LAVENDER BAGS

Really simple: To make a lavender bag that requires no sewing, choose a pretty napkin in a porous fabric like linen, loosely woven cotton, or organza. Pour the lavender flowers into the center of the napkin and tie with matching or contrasting ribbons.

Truly simple: Cut four pieces of fabric—embroidered organza, moire, printed linen—and make two small pillows. Leave open on one end. Fill with lavender flowers. Stitch shut. Decorate with ribbon and silk flowers.

Medium simple: Take a light linen or organza handkerchief and fold it on the diagonal. Fold the two sides in to make an envelope. Stitch along the sides and bottom. Fill the envelope with lavender and fold over the top flap. Sew shut or glue with a hot glue gun. Sew or glue flowers or bows for decoration.

A Victorian Retreat

Victoria MacKenzie-Childs says that the laundry room in her nineteenth-century upstate New York farmhouse is her favorite room in the entire house. She retreats to this room to design the pattern-upon-pattern china, linens, and furniture that bear her name. "I have filled this room with so many of my favorite things," she says. "It is a pleasure to work here."

Victoria has a large collection of antique linens that she enjoys mending, washing, and pressing in this room. She still uses the vintage mangle to iron her linen towels and cotton sheets.

The old stone walls of Victoria's basement laundry room have been covered with plaster but they still have that rustic look. She displays her tole trays and antique plates on a smooth, interior wall. Vintage enamelware pots and buckets hang from the ceiling. Grouping collections of similar objects makes a very effective display.

How to Get the Look

When planning your laundry room, ask yourself if you want it to be in its traditional place in the basement. Do you want it on the first floor where, perhaps, it can also serve as a mudroom? Do you want a laundry room on the second floor where, after all, most of the laundry is generated if your bedrooms and at least one bathroom are on that floor?

Would you like a spacious laundry room where you can sort, pretreat, and fold clothing? Would you also like a room with large windows in which to sew, iron, and do crafts? Perhaps you would like the laundry to double as a household office.

A successful room has to be both useful and inviting.

Karen Moore from Djuna says, "Decide how much storage space you think you will need, double that amount, and you will come out just about right."

"Make it colorful and playful," says Victoria MacKenzie-Childs. "Make it the most fun room in your home. Remember that laundry rooms are not just for laundry anymore."

Moths are mightily attracted to the odor of wool, cashmere, and other animal hair fibers. As an extra treat, they love the salts and oils of sweat and grease. That's why you get all those holes in your sweaters. Keeping moths from making their homes in your winter woolens is not difficult if you make the proper repellent. The trick is to make a moth chaser that doesn't repel people. Many strongly scented herbs (used singly or layered with others) are ideal for the job.

Here are some recipes for keeping moths out of your woolen clothes and blankets—without resorting to camphor moth balls.

Tie a few sprigs of fresh herbs like lavender, rosemary, lemon verbena, or thyme in among the clothes you put away for the summer.

To make moth bags, simply make "little pillowcases" about 3 inches by 5 inches, using porous fabric such as cheesecloth, muslin, or linen. Tie the bags with a looped string for hanging over a closet hook or hanger.

MAKING MOTH BAGS

The trick is to make strongly scented moth-chaser bags that repel moths and other insects but don't also repel people.

A household hints book published by the Ladies of Monte Vista, Colorado, in 1927 says to mix 1 ounce each of ground cloves, nutmeg, cinnamon, mace, and caraway seeds with 6 ounces of powdered orrisroot. Put this in little moth bags.

Another potent mixture is 2 ounces lavender, 2 ounces southernwood, 1 ounce rosemary, 1 ounce black pepper, and 1 ounce of ground cloves. Mix well. Put into moth bags.

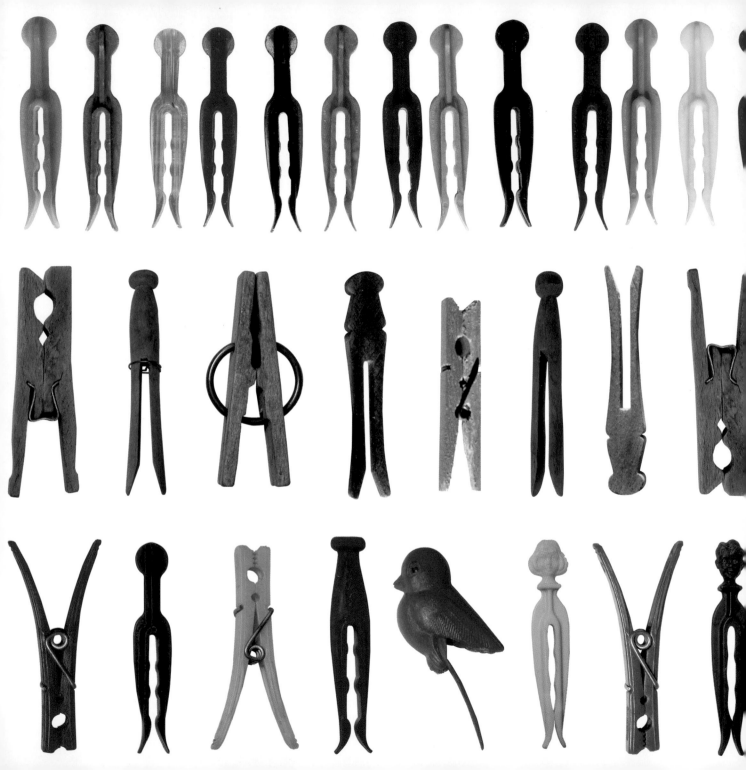

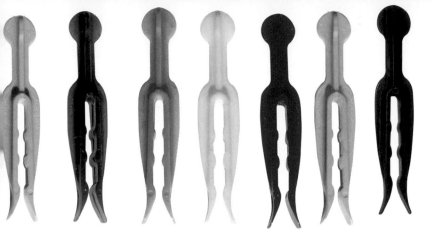

Everyone collects something—matchbooks and menus, salt and pepper shakers shaped like deer or ducks, tin wind-up toys, old fishing gear, or vintage postcards with views of state monuments and national parks.

Collectibles don't have to be antiques, although many of them have acquired the patina of age. They don't have to be validated by shows in museums, although many of them have. Their market value is not set by art galleries or art dealers; it comes from the passion with which they are sought by novice and experienced collectors who get up before dawn to be the first at a flea market or swap meet. Market value also depends on the design, material, age, authenticity, and condition of each object.

As more people have become interested in decorating their laundry rooms, clothesline collectibles are beginning to attract attention in antiques shops and on eBay. Everything—from embroidered laundry bags to simple wooden clothespins, from early laborsaving devices to vintage boxes of detergent—is snapped up. Some collectibles are refurbished and returned to their original use. Others are displayed as objet d'art.

Another Time, Another Place

There was a time when the clothesline was a metaphor understood by all. Everyone washed clothes and everyone hung them out on the line. Name brands like Buick, Pepsi, and Zenith used the clothesline in their advertising to symbolize cleanliness, wholesomeness, and a job well done.

The clothesline appeared on humorous postcards available in gift shops and drugstores in the 1940s and 1950s. They were sent by vacationers to the Florida coast, sailors on leave during World War II, and anyone else who wanted to send home a short lighthearted greeting. These cards are increasingly rare and are highly prized by collectors of paper ephemera.

A portable clothesline with a nautical theme, *above*, comes neatly organized in its own tin traveling box. The postcard, *left*, is typical of those sent home by servicemen during World War II. The cover of *Buick* magazine, *right*, shows a young woman hanging out the wash on a windy day.

BUICK Magazine

MARCH 1941

VOLUME 6 · NUMBER 12

Price, 10 cents

Bare & Decorated Necessities

Not many people spend a lot of time thinking about clothespins. After all, they are only small pieces of wood or plastic meant to keep wet clothes attached to a line. To collectors they are much more. They search for unusual or hand-made wooden pins. Plastic pins with animal or human heads, or shaped like birds, fish, or little sprigs of holly (designed to hold Christmas cards on a string) are especially desirable. Bakelite clothespins in faded colors like sage green, summer-porch blue, Chinese red, and soft amber are lovely but expensive and difficult to find.

To learn about the history of the clothespin, and to see clothespins that are more than a century old, including models of the nation's first patented clothespins, visit the Museum of American Art (part of the Smithsonian Institution) in Washington, D.C.

Early spring-clip wooden clothes-pins, *above*, are becoming rare. Children hanging up the laundry was a popular motif on dishes, *left*, and handkerchiefs, *facing*. Laundry bags come in many shapes and sizes—many embroidered or embellished with color-fast paints.

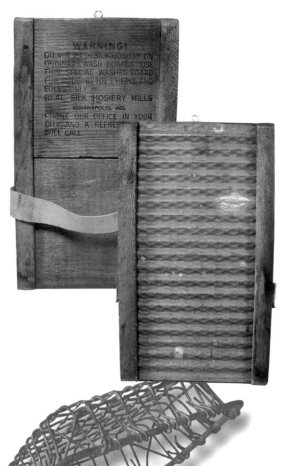

Laborsaving Devices

As long as people have being doing laundry, other people have been inventing laborsaving devices to make doing the wash seem like less of a chore. Some of these devices are still useful today. Others have become as obsolete as the buggy whip.

One of the earliest inventions—even before the hand-cranked washing machine—was the washboard, a giant step up from pounding the laundry against stones in the river. Time passed and the washboards graduated from being made out of galvanized iron to glass. But, even in the days of an automatic washer, women continued to wash their delicates like silk stockings with the help of a washboard. Responding to this, manufacturers made small, portable boards.

Stretchers for socks, gloves, hats, and trousers were popular because, if they were

A small washboard, *upper left*, has an elastic strap for easy handling and printed instructions on the back. The wire object, *left*, is a soap saver and the item, *above top*, is a sock stretcher. Early clothesline winders, *right*, are very collectible. The wooden object, *facing*, *above right*, is a stretcher made specifically for the fingers of kid gloves. Mrs. Stewart's Liquid Bluing, *facing*, *lower right*, made whites whiter.

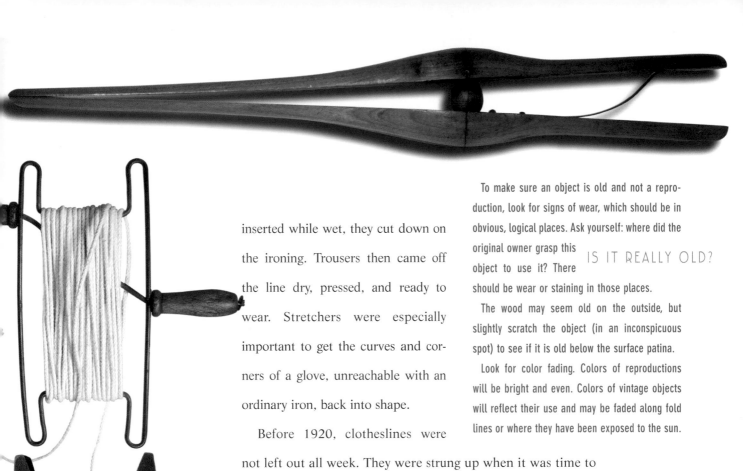

inserted while wet, they cut down on the ironing. Trousers then came off the line dry, pressed, and ready to wear. Stretchers were especially important to get the curves and corners of a glove, unreachable with an ordinary iron, back into shape.

Before 1920, clotheslines were not left out all week. They were strung up when it was time to do the wash on Monday and taken down after the wash was dry. To leave them out at the mercy of the elements would have been wasteful, so devices were invented to wind up and put away the clothesline when it was not in use. Most were primitive wooden or iron objects. Some seem unnecessarily complicated to put together and operate until you realize that the 1800s and 1900s included the age of invention.

To make sure an object is old and not a reproduction, look for signs of wear, which should be in obvious, logical places. Ask yourself: where did the original owner grasp this object to use it? There should be wear or staining in those places.

IS IT REALLY OLD?

The wood may seem old on the outside, but slightly scratch the object (in an inconspicuous spot) to see if it is old below the surface patina.

Look for color fading. Colors of reproductions will be bright and even. Colors of vintage objects will reflect their use and may be faded along fold lines or where they have been exposed to the sun.

Showing Off

Finding and buying vintage clothesline collectibles is only half the fun. Displaying your collection is the other half. The walls and shelves of a newly redecorated laundry room are the perfect place, but so are many other rooms in your home. Arrange boxes and cans of unopened soap powder, starch, and bluing on a shelf in your kitchen. Hang some primitive laborsaving devices, like wire soap savers or glove and sock stretchers, on a wall in your bathroom.

Frame a grouping of twenty colorful plastic or Bakelite clothespins by color—using their subtle shadings and fadings to create a rainbow-like composition. First attach them to foam core or poster board with straight pins or, if you want the arrangement to be permanent, use a hot glue gun.

The wall over a bed or bureau is the perfect place to display a collection of hand-embroidered laundry bags. They can also be used to store small, light objects like scarves, stockings, and handkerchiefs. Hanging them from a clothesline adds an extra element of whimsy.

Grouping similar objects close together gives a sense of abundance and makes your collection look larger. Use color, shape, and original use as a guide. On a shelf, the larger objects go in back. On a wall, hang the larger objects lower and smaller ones higher. This makes a more pleasing composition.

DECORATING DETAILS

Repeating a single graphic element, like a simple clothespin, can make a very contemporary artistic statement. Consider framing plain wooden clothespins in two precisely lined-up rows of three each.

the dirt out!

Then let your clothes soak in this sudsy Rinso an hour—over night if you wish—then give them a good thorough rinse and out they come spotlessly clean—shining white and sweet.

Table cloths, towels, sheets, all those bulky pieces so heavy to drag up and down on the washboard are soaked snowy white in the rich Rinso suds.

Even hard-to-get-at dirt on seats and knees of little rompers or badly ground-in, grimy cuff edges and collar bands take only a light rubbing to get them as white as new.

Of course you have your own special way of doing your wash—every woman has—but whatever method you use, Rinso gives you what you've always wanted—a laundry soap that does a *thorough job* in the most up-to-date way—the way that saves your time and energy.

It is perfect for every kind of washing machine; nothing could be better for boiling white cottons; and it is simply wonderful for soaking.

At every step of the family wash you just use Rinso instead of old-fashioned bar soap. You need no other soap if you use Rinso. It does the whole job.

Rinso is made by the makers of Lux, the largest soap-makers in the world. They spared no effort of testing or research to make Rinso meet every modern need for a perfect laundry soap—just as Lux meets today's need for a special soap for all fine things.

Do your next wash with Rinso. Get it from your grocer—a big new package or the regular size. Lever Bros. Co., Cambridge, Mass.

❦

If you have a washing machine, follow the advice of these leading makers "Use RINSO"

APEX	MEADOWS
BLUEBIRD	"1900" CATARACT
COFFIELD	ONE MINUTE
GAINADAY	ROTAREX
GETZ	SAVAGE
HORTON	SUNBEAM SURF-ACTION
LAUN-DRY-ETTE	SUNNYSUDS

After so *easy* a wash you have "pep" enough left to romp with the youngsters

One important point is to use enough Rinso to get big lasting suds after the clothes have been put in

SOAKING · BOILING · WASHING MACHINE—
Use RINSO

Advertising Age

The bright colors and bold graphics of vintage advertising posters have long attracted collectors. Ads touting the latest inventions—from soap powders to washing machines, from scented starches to laundry baskets—also crowded the pages of early- and mid-twentieth-century women's magazines. This is a good place for beginning collectors to look. Find vintage issues of *Hearth & Home, Ladies' Home Journal, Woman's Day, Good Housekeeping, House Beautiful* or other magazines geared toward women; leaf through the pages and you will find dozens of laundry-related ads.

Choose the pages that appeal to you and cut them out of the magazines using a mat-knife (available in art-supply stores). Mat in acid-free paper. Frame identically and hang symmetrically. An entire wall can be decorated quickly and effectively this way.

Remember that a grouping of similar objects—all massed together—creates the illusion of abundance, making your collection look bigger and more dramatic.

Old advertisements cut out of vintage women's magazines or peeled off old cans of soap and bleach can add interest to a laundry room, bathroom, or kitchen wall. For framing, choose several in colors, sizes, and themes that are compatible. For a less expensive alternative, laminate the ads in plastic and, using colorful clothespins, hang them on a line on the wall.

So many artists—from well-knowns like J. Alden Weir and Alice Neel, to lesser-knowns like Betsy Bennett and Bob Ragland —have featured clotheslines in their oils, watercolors, charcoal drawings, and pastels. Why? Each artist tells a similar story: fascination with the play of light and shadow, with the motion created by the wind, with the shimmer of damp garments in the sunlight, with the classical drape of towels and sheets.

Starting with the Impressionists (both French and American) in the late 1800s and early 1900s, artists have found beauty in the smallest and most commonplace things. A pot of chives, an old oaken bucket, a load of laundry flapping in the wind—all were appreciated for their simple, honest beauty.

"You never really look carefully at the world until you start to paint it," says artist Betsy Bennett. "I know this sounds funny, but I think of hanging clothes as an almost religious experience. Being a mother, it epitomizes to me the link between all mothers. When you think of it, a clothesline is really symbolic of so many things."

Sheets to the Wind II
egg tempera, 8 x 12 in.
Betsy Bennett

Laundry in Winter
watercolor, 9 x 12 in.
James Ames

A Simple, Honest Beauty

J. Alden Weir, one of the American Impressionists, painted the everyday scenes he found on his farm in Connecticut. The long, sloping lawn leading up to the back of the farmhouse was a favorite subject—especially on wash day when long lines of clothes hanging out to dry gave motion to the landscape.

The stark clothesline in winter, above, is typical of James Ames's early work. His Andrew Wyeth–like paintings, done with a broodingly lonely brush, are always blushed by an unexpected touch of color—like the red long johns. We are reminded that winter's snowy cloak gives ordinary objects a new importance.

e Laundry, Branchville, c. 1894
on canvas,
⅛ x 25 ¼ in.
Alden Weir

Frozen Stiff

Bob Ragland always carries brushes, paints, and a small easel in the backseat of his car because he never knows when he will find a landscape or cityscape to paint. He remembers painting this small oil without getting out of the car. "It was a bright day but so cold, the entire line was frozen stiff," says Bob.

He continues: "I've always been fond of clotheslines because I remember my mother with clothespins in her mouth . . . hanging out the wash. She made lye soap and stretched the lace living room curtains on a wooden stretcher to dry."

*The Laundry at Fourth
and Grant, Denver, 1989.*
oil on canvas, 9 x 12 in.
Bob Ragland

Alice Neel lived in a tiny Brooklyn walk-up and everything she saw outside her windows was fodder for her art. Her bold and unique style stripped away all prettiness and pretension and got right down to the basics. Her painting of laundry hung out on the fire escape shows us a clothesline of necessity.

Fire Escape, 1948
oil on canvas, 34 x 25 in.
Alice Neel

Summer in the City

Urban clotheslines have to coexist with satellite dishes, water tanks, and pigeon coops. It takes talent to hang a cramped city line. A three-foot piece of line holds an entire week's laundry, sometimes hung in layers—heavier clothes on the bottom, lighter ones on top. Often the line is strung from one side of a small balcony to the other and back again, like the childrens' string game "Cat's Cradle."

There's a certain vulnerability embodied in all inner-city clotheslines. Close neighbors can see every tear, spot, and stain. There's also an irrepressible hopefulness. Urban photographers capture this on film, painters on canvas.

Courtyard Clothesline
color photograph, 8 x 10 in.
James O. Milmoe

HINTS FOR PHOTOGRAPHERS

- Even if you only have a point-and-shoot camera, you can take some excellent clothesline photographs. Ask permission first.
- Mondays will likely give you the most choices.
- Start with the sun at your back. This guarantees a good picture. Then shoot straight toward the sun so the light shines through the clothes, creating interesting light and shadow.
- Try different angles. Get under the clothesline and shoot toward the sky.
- Get dramatic close-ups of clothespins, laundry bags, and individual pieces of laundry.

Hanging Out
oil on canvas, 12 x 16 in.
Frances Gottlieb

Dirt Roads and Neat Lines

Dirt roads and two-lane highways passing through small country towns are still the best places to see laundry out on the line, according to contemporary *plein air* artists. Frances Gottlieb gets in her car and drives until she sees something she wants to paint. "Mondays are good days to get on the road," she says. "The tradition of doing the wash on Mondays is still very strong in rural areas . . . and women are careful to make their lines look really good because they know that folks are looking at them."

AFFORDING ART

- You don't have to take out a bank loan to buy art.
- Check with the Art Students' League or your local arts high school for sales of student work. Be patient. You might to have look at a lot of bad art to find the gems.
- Check with the mayor's or governor's office in your town and state. There's usually a department of art and culture that has a registry of local artists.
- Make appointments to visit artists in their studios. Ask if they have a payment plan.
- Some great finds have been made at tag sales, garage sales, and church rummage sales.

Summer Garden
watercolor, 20 x 16 in.
Susan Elliott

A folk-art hooked rug, *above*, by Maine artist Barbara Merry shows laundry day outside a little log cabin. Nostalgic wash-day needlework designs——needle-point on canvas, *facing, upper right* and cross-stitch on cotton fabric, *facing, lower right*——are excellent decorative elements in a country home.

Clothesline Crafts

Clothesline-inspired crafts are popular—needle-point, cross stitch, and even hooked-rug patterns are inspired by clothes hanging out on a line. Rug-maker Barbara Merry lives in Belfast, Maine, one of those small coastal towns that tourist guides describe as picturesque and unspoiled. For more than thirty years she has transformed scrap fabric and burlap into folk-art rugs. She has lived in Maine most of her life and the rugs she makes are usually autobio-graphical. Laundry in the Merry household was always done on Monday—in fair weather or foul. The laundry lines of her childhood often appear in the burlap and wool art she creates for the floor.

Clothespin Toys

In previous, more frugal generations—particularly in rural households—fathers and grandfathers made toys out of simple, everyday things. Clothespins were one of their favorite raw materials—providing an endless supply of lumber from which to create doll furniture. Because clothespins were cheap, it was possible to surprise a child on Christmas morning with a whole row of porch chairs, a four-poster bed, or a complete dining room set for mere pennies.

You can still find these lovingly made chairs and rockers in thrift stores or you can buy them newly made from country crafts-people like Bill Hall in Waldeboro, Maine. Another alternative is to make them yourself using the spring or straight knob-top

Colorful chairs and rockers, *below*, are made from disassembled spring clothespins. The dollies' tea party, *facing*, takes place on furniture made from knob-top clothespins. The dark-haired doll is made entirely out of clothespins.

clothespins. There really aren't any set patterns—just get some clothespins and a hot glue gun. Then look at the photographs and use your imagination. If your creations are a little irregular, a little folk-arty, that will only add to their charm.

Here are some of our favorite clothesline-related sources.

2 peas in a pod
800-HBENDEL
www.2peasinapod.com
*Frangipani-scented laundry wash
and linen water.*

Aboyne Linen and Lace
Box 340
Elora, ON Canada N0B 1S0
888.822.6963
www.aboynelinen.com
Antique and vintage linen.

James Ames
3201 Salishan Circle
Flint, MI 48506
Member American Watercolor Society
Watercolors, illustrations and design.

Betsy Bennett
Frog Pond Studio
240 Chatham Road
Harwich, MA 02645
508.430.0264
Cape Cod artist.

Best of New England
370 Cedar Avenue
East Greenwich, RI 02818
800.891.8644
www.bestofnewengland.com
Red cedar clothespins.

Canterbury Designs
Box 204060
Martinez, GA 30917
706.860.1674
cdxs@home.com
Cross-stitch design.

Cross My Heart
4725 Commercial Drive NW
Huntsville, AL 35816
256.721.1431
Cross-stitch design.

Delaware City Soap Company
P.O. Box 4112
Delaware City, DE 19706
302.832.2469
www.delcitysoap.com
Specialty soaps.

**De Le Cuona Textile
and Home Collection**
The Old Stables
9-10 Osbourne Mews
Windsor, Berkshire
England SL4 3DE
44.(0)1753.830.301
www.delecuona.co.uk
*Antique paisley shawls,
cashmere pillows and blankets,
linen duvet covers and throws.*

Diamond Brands, Inc.
1800 Cloquet Avenue
Cloquet, MN 55720
800.777.7942
www.diamondbrands.com
Manufacturer of clothespins.

Dining & Company
Box 182
Lawrenceville, IL 62439
800.747.5479
www.dining-company.com
Sparkle detergent and laundry-room art.

Djuna
221 Detroit Street
Denver, CO 80206
303.355.3500
www.djuna.com
*Art, antiques, fabrics,
unique home furnishings.*

Enchante Accessories
4 East 34th Street, #4
New York, NY 10016
212.689.6008
Parisian home-laundry powder.

FarmBid.Com
4 West Olas Boulevard, Suite 203
Ft. Lauderdale, FL 33301
954.761.9677
www.farmbid.com
Clotheslines and accessories.

Good Home Company
134 West 26th Street
New York, NY 10001
888.GHC.2862
www.goodhomeco.com
Lavender dryer bags and linen spray.

Goodwin Creek Gardens
Box 83
Williams, OR 97544
800.846.7359
www.goodwincreekgardens.com
Fresh and dried lavender.

Frances Gottlieb
frang@qwest.net
Outdoor landscape painter.

GreenMarketplace.Com
5801 Beacon Street, Suite 2
Pittsburgh, PA 15217
888.59.EARTH
www.greenmarketplace.com
*Organically grown and produced
laundry soap, detergent, and fabric softener.*

William Hall
whallsr@ny.tds.net
Folk-art clothespin chairs and rockers.

Hold Everything
7720 NW 85th Terrace
Oklahoma City, OK 73132
800.421.2264
Laundry supplies and accessories.

IMM International
P.O. Box 15580
Durham, NC 27704
866.485-9464
www.clothesdrying.com
Gull-wing collapsible drying racks.

Jade Mountain, Inc.
360 Interlocken Boulevard, Suite 300
Broomfield, CO 80021
800.442.1972
www.jademountain.com
Clotheslines and laundry racks.

**The Laundry at
Linens Limited, Inc.**
240 North Milwaukee Street
Milwaukee, WI 53202
800.637.6334
Expert lace cleaning and restoration.

MacKenzie-Childs, Ltd.
824 Madison Avenue
New York, NY 10021
212.570.6050
www.mackenzie-childs.com
Whimsical home furnishings.

Martha by Mail
Box 30676
Tampa, FL 33630-0676
800.950.7130
www.marthastewart.com
*Clothespin bags, irons, ironing
boards, laundry room storage.*

May Arts
1154 East Putnam Avenue
Riverside, CT 06878
203.637.8366
Fine silk ribbon.

Barbara Merry
Smart Road
Belfast, ME 04915
207.338.6571
Handmade folk-art rugs.

James O. Milmoe
14900 Foothill Road
Golden, CO 80401
303.279.4364
jim@milmoe.com
Photography.

Odalisque
7278 Beverly Boulevard
Los Angeles, CA 90036
323.933.9100
Antique 100-percent-cotton linens.

Planet Sack
1320 West 12th Place
Los Angeles, CA 90015
213.745.4544
*Sheer silk sacks for making lavender
and other herb sachet bags.*

Project Laundry List
P.O. Box 189
South Royalton, VT 05068
802.234.5988
www.laundrylist.org
*Best place on the web for
laundry-related questions.*

Purple Haze Lavender
180 Bell Bottom Road
Sequim, WA 98382
888.852.6560
www.purplehazelavender.com
Fresh and dried lavender.

Rabbit Shadow Farms
2880 East Highway 402
Loveland, CO 80537
800.850.5531
Lavender plants, topiaries.

Bob Ragland
1723 East 25th Avenue
Denver, CO 80205
303.839.5259
bogragland@hotmail.com
Landscapes and cityscapes in oil.

Restoration Hardware
www.restorationhardware.com
Laundry-room accessories.

Robert Miller Gallery
The Alice Neel Estate
524 West 26th Street
New York, NY 10001
www.robertmillergallery.com
Fine art.

Rowenta
196 Boston Avenue
Medford, MA 02155
781.396.0600
www.rowentausa.com
High-performance irons.

Rue de France
78 Thames Street
Newport, RI 02840
800.777.0998
www.ruedefrance.com
French laundry powder.

SunFeather Natural Soap Co.
1551 State Highway 72
Potsdam, NY 13676
315.265.3648
www.sunsoap.com
Natural soaps, soapmaking ingredients.

Vintage Linen Warehouse
Box 1607
North Kingstown, RI 02852
www.vintagelinen.com
Vintage linens.

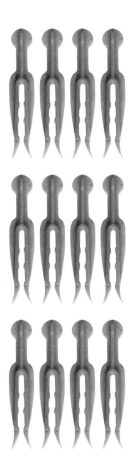

Acknowledgements—*Many, many thanks to friends, neighbors, and, in some cases, total strangers, who allowed us to invade their private spaces and photograph their clothes drying out on the line. We are especially grateful to Sharon Boucher of Avalanche Ranch, Karen Moore of Djuna, Victoria MacKenzie-Childs, Darla Worden, Sandra Dallas, Bo and Kay Ivanovic, and Debbie Geiger. Many, many thanks to Mary Abel for patiently providing so much assistance. Thanks also to Tammy Richards, Donna Pacheco, Crystal Reid, Sanya Kushak, Carol Showell, Loneta Daniel and Pat Kowalewski. Finally, we would like to thank our editor, Suzanne Taylor, for support, encouragement, and the occasional kick in the pants.*

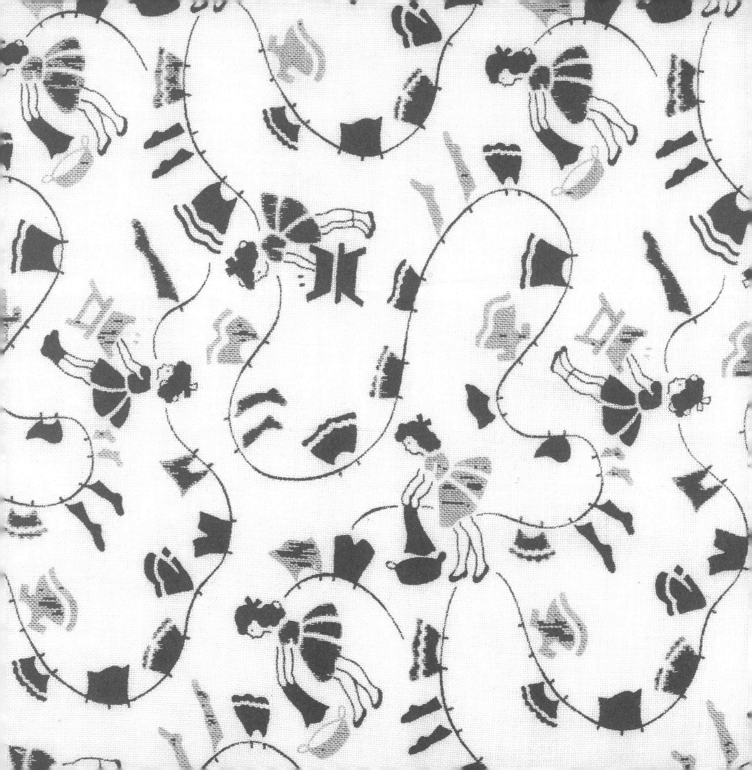

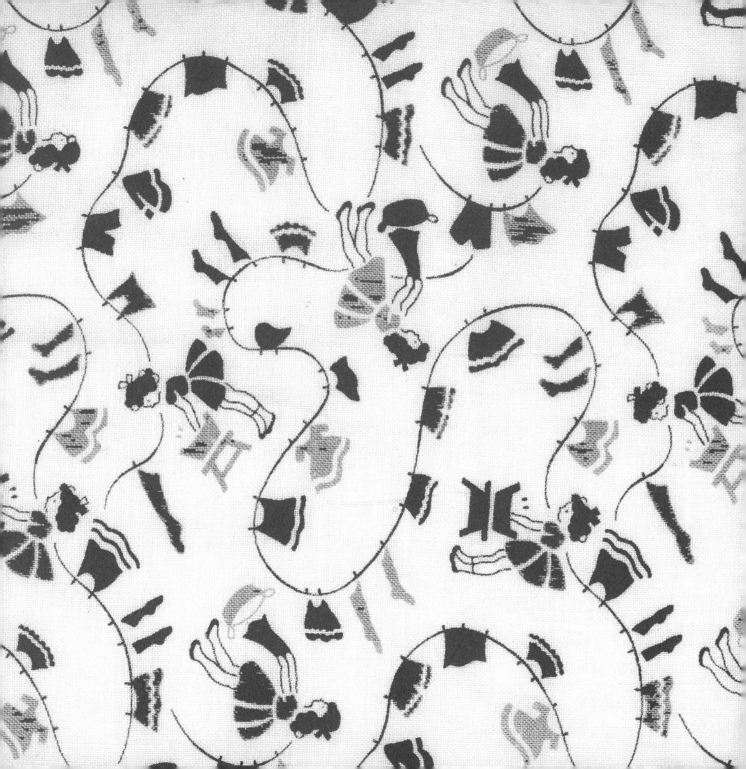